WRITE THIS WAY

WRITING NOTABLE NARRATIVE NONFICTION

SUE VANDER HOOK

LERNER PUBLICATIONS ◆ MINNEAPOLIS

Lerner Publications Company
A division of Lerner Publishing Group, Inc.
241 First Avenue North
Minneapolis, MN 55401 USA

For reading levels and more information, look up this title at www.lernerbooks.com.

Main body text set in Dante MT Std 12/15. Typeface provided by Monotype.

Library of Congress Cataloging-in-Publication Data

Vander Hook, Sue, 1949–
    Writing notable narrative nonfiction / by Sue Vander Hook.
    pages cm. — (Write this way)
    ISBN 978-1-4677-8084-1 (lb : alk. paper) — ISBN 978-1-4677-8292-0 (pb : alk. paper) — ISBN 978-1-4677-8293-7 (eb pdf)
    1. Authorship—Juvenile literature. 2. Narration (Rhetoric)—Juvenile literature. 3. Creative nonfiction—Authorship—Juvenile literature. I. Title.
PN159.V36 2016
808.02—dc23   2014045236

Manufactured in the United States of America
1 – VP – 7/15/15

Table of Contents

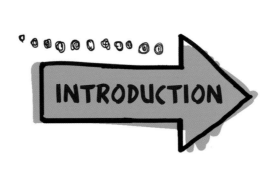

INTRODUCTION

Release the writer inside you! Perhaps you've always wanted to write but you've convinced yourself that you're just not a writer. That's not true! If you have thoughts and ideas and stories in your head, you *are* a writer. You just haven't taken them out of your brain and put them on paper—yet.

Maybe you already write a lot. You've written poems or fiction, and now you'd like to try something new. **The word** ***nonfiction*** **in the title of this book might have caught your eye. You might be interested in finding out whether writing about true events is up your alley.**

Regardless of where you are on your writing journey, remember that everyone, including you, has a true story to tell. So don't be afraid to dive into nonfiction writing. After all, if you leave your story inside your head, with time, it could become just a jumble of random events and people that don't make much sense. Writing down your story will give it meaning and value—to you *and* to anyone who reads it.

Also know that no story is too small or insignificant to tell. Someone once asked author John Green, of *The Fault in Our Stars* fame, where he gets ideas for his books. "Well, my books don't have capital-i Ideas, really," he answered. "I don't have ideas that hit like a ton of bricks out of nowhere, like BAM! . . . The ideas for my books come from lowercase-i ideas . . . little ideas will come along and link up to other little ideas." Sometimes little ideas and simple stories make for the very best kind of writing.

So what's in *your* head? What are you interested in? Perhaps real events in history energize you. Maybe you're even one of those amazing people who can "see" history like an exciting movie. Or you may have personal memories lurking in your mind that you'd like to share. Have you been internally replaying the tale of your favorite vacation over and over? What about that tragedy in your life? Have you told anyone how it made you feel? Would your story help someone struggling with the same issue? And what about your favorite (or not-so-favorite) person? He or she could also make for a pretty good story.

You don't have to write fiction to make a story interesting. Many people enjoy reading true stories just as much as made-up ones. In fact, one of the fastest-growing genres today is narrative nonfiction. Lee Gutkind, founder of *Creative Nonfiction* magazine, defined the genre best. According to him, it's "true stories well told." He explains that in good narrative nonfiction writing, "the goal is to make nonfiction stories read like fiction so that your readers are as enthralled by fact as they are by fantasy."

That's where you, the writer, come into the picture. You become a wordsmith to make your story come alive. Through the clever use of the five senses, similes, metaphors, personification, and more, you can turn simple facts into an interesting tale that will capture the reader's attention.

This book will guide you through the process of writing narrative nonfiction, from beginning to end. You'll start by discovering a topic. Next, you'll gather facts, chart your course, and break through what haunts almost every writer: writer's block. Then you'll write a bad first draft. (We're not insulting your writing skills. Most writers' first drafts are bad—and that's perfectly fine!) Finally, you'll learn how to review and revise your writing, which includes being your own editor. You'll incorporate feedback from others too. The result will be a really good story.

Now it's time to get started on your writing adventure. So get ready to tell a true story—and to tell it well!

DISCOVER A TOPIC

So what true story should you tell? Your first step in writing narrative nonfiction is choosing a topic. That's probably not a surprise. If you're going to write, you need something to write about! When it comes to choosing a topic for your nonfiction piece, some people say writing what you know is the way to go. These people tell about their own experiences and the people they've met. They set scenes and provide details to draw readers in. They write about themselves. The key is to write about ordinary places and regular people in an interesting way.

That's exactly what Sandra Cisneros did for her first novel, *The House on Mango Street*. Cisneros's ordinary topic was the people in her neighborhood. While the story is fiction, Cisneros relied on her own real-life experiences growing up to write it, including having six brothers, a Mexican American mother, and a Mexican father who often moved the family between Chicago and Mexico City. Writing her book taught Cisneros a lot about herself:

> *It wasn't as if I didn't know who I was. I knew I was a Mexican woman. But, I didn't think it had anything to do with why I felt so much imbalance in my life, whereas it had everything to do with it! My race, my gender, and my class! . . . That's when I decided I would write about something [many others] couldn't write about.*

LEARN FROM THE MASTERS

Some of the most admired authors have written about their own lives. Jeannette Walls (below), author of *The Glass Castle: A Memoir*, used her own difficult childhood as the topic of her book. "At one point, I tried to fictionalize it," Walls admitted, "but that didn't work."

For years, she tried to write her story, but she always threw it away. "Getting at the truth isn't all that easy," she said. When Walls decided to tell the whole truth about her past, which includes moving around a lot and having an alcoholic father, Walls finished her first draft in only six weeks and found the experience to be a good one. "*The Glass Castle* allowed me to be honest about who I really am," she said.

CONSIDER THE POSSIBILITIES

Everyone—and, yes, that means you too!—has something to write about. It may be ordinary. It may be extraordinary. Think about an event or a person you can transform into a stunning, interesting story. Or maybe a part of your life stands out to you. Think about experiences you've had—funny, embarrassing, or even something that still hurts a lot. Those experiences and the people who were part of them have taken up residence in your head and are waiting to get out. You just need to put the stories on paper.

Award-winning nonfiction writer Joan Didion did just that after her husband died suddenly. The result was a nonfiction book titled *The Year of Magical Thinking*. She started it this way: "Life changes fast. Life changes in the instant. You sit down to dinner and life as you know it ends." She shared a very personal, painful event in a way that revealed her deepest emotions about the experience, which helps her connect with readers.

Didion's book is one example of how the bumps of life can make for interesting reading. **In addition, writing about personal challenges can be cathartic, a way of processing what happened and getting through it.** As you search for a topic, you might think about challenges in your own life that you could write about.

Of course, writing about yourself isn't required. Not all narrative nonfiction is autobiographical. A work of narrative nonfiction can also be about an incident in history, such as the sinking of the *Titanic* or the terrorist attacks that took place in the United States on September 11, 2001. The key to narrative nonfiction is telling a true story, and the list of possible topics is endless. That can make deciding on a topic challenging. So given all the options, just how do you pick a topic? Brainstorming is often a good place to start.

BRAINSTORM IDEAS

Have you brainstormed before? It's easy. Brainstorming involves throwing out ideas—really, anything that comes to mind. You can use different methods to brainstorm. Here are suggestions for two methods. You'll need a notebook and a pen or pencil. Or if you prefer to use a computer or tablet, working electronically is definitely an option for the first method. So grab a notebook or the electronic device of your choice and get ready to let your ideas flow.

First, divide the page into four columns. Give the columns these headings:

Column 1: *Personal experiences (some happy, some painful)*
Column 2: *People I've known (or want to know)*
Column 3: *Places I've been (or would like to visit)*
Column 4: *Historical events that rock (or trouble me)*

Next, fill the columns with anything that comes to mind. Try to generate ten items for each category. If you come up with more than ten, that's great. You'll simply have that many more possible topics to choose from. No topic is too ridiculous to write down, so try not to censor yourself. Just get as much as you can out of your head and into your notebook or on your device.

Once you've hit at least the ten-item minimum for each column, take a break. Walk away from your lists for five to ten minutes. When you come back, circle or highlight one topic in each column that stands out, for four total, and then walk away for a while again. When you come back this time, choose one topic out of the four that you're most passionate about. That might be the topic of your narrative nonfiction piece.

For the second brainstorming method, grab a notebook. Begin by drawing a circle in the center of a blank page in the notebook. In that circle, write down something you're interested in. **Being interested is important. You'll be more enthusiastic about the topic and more likely to want to write about it than you would a topic you aren't really interested in.**

Next, draw about ten lines radiating from the circle to make what look like rays of the sun. Armed with your paper and pencil, ask anyone to write down what he or she knows or would like to know about your topic. This could be parents, grandparents, siblings, friends, classmates, teachers—even the clerk at the grocery store. Each person gets one or two spokes.

Once you've finished gathering thoughts from others, get another sheet of paper and repeat this process with a different topic in the center circle. After you've completed the second round of input, sit down and read what everyone wrote about your topics. You'll be amazed at how many ideas other people can give you.

Which topic is shouting, "Write about me!" from the page? The standout topic might be the one you wrote in the center circle, it may be something a person wrote on one of the spokes, or it could even be a new idea that came up as a result of reading what others wrote. Maybe more than one topic stands out. Which one of the standout topics do you like most? That would probably be a great thing to write about.

If you just can't decide on a topic, you can try this: write your standout topics on pieces of paper, one topic per piece, and then put the pieces in a bag, shake the bag to mix them, reach in, and grab one. Ta-da! Whatever's written on the piece of paper you chose is your topic. If you decide you *really* don't want to write about that subject, just pull out another piece of paper.

Once you discover your topic, get ready. You're about to do your first bit of writing for your nonfiction narrative.

CREATE A (TEMPORARY) TITLE

You've thought and brainstormed and settled on a topic. You're ready for your first piece of writing. It's a short but important one. On a blank computer page or at the top of a sheet of notebook paper, type or write the title of your narrative nonfiction piece. Of course, that title will probably change a bunch of times throughout this process, but writing it down will mark an important step. You've started your story. You've begun your journey to writing narrative nonfiction. Congratulations!

Keep moving forward. The next step is to gather resources and facts—you need details for your story. Onward!

WRITE IT OUT!
Once you've chosen your topic, get a large sheet of paper and a marker. As quickly as you can, fill the paper with words that have anything to do with the topic you've chosen—nouns, verbs, adjectives, or whatever you like. The goal is to flood your brain with words that relate to your topic. You'll probably be able to use a lot of these words in your narrative nonfiction piece.

COLLECT THE FACTS

You're off to a great start! Now it's time to collect facts. You want to find some good sources for information to add to your piece. There are all kinds of sources, including your own brain. The library and the Internet are definite go-to resources. There are other options too. Keep reading to find out more. And get ready to do some serious digging for facts.

THINK AND ASK

If your topic is a personal experience, your memory is one of the main resources for your narrative nonfiction piece. If your topic isn't personal, you still may know something about it. After all, the topic attracted you.

Using a pen and paper or a device, write down anything you remember or know about your topic. Write whatever comes to mind. Stay with it until you fill up the whole page.

On a second page, write a lot of questions to yourself. **Think about what you still need to know about your topic to make your narrative nonfiction interesting.** Fill up the page with any questions you can think of—no question is too basic to ask. If you know someone who might be able to answer a question, put that person's name next to it.

EXPLORE, INVESTIGATE, PROBE

Once you've pulled out everything possible from your brain, it's time to do some research. For some people, doing research may not sound very fun. But really, it can be quite interesting. There's just so much to know about so many things. You'll likely uncover all kinds of great information—some of it will be useful for your story, and some of it will just be fun to know.

Exploring print resources and the Internet should provide a wealth of possibilities. **You may want to start with print resources at the library. These materials could help you with your Internet search.** You may, for example, find a book or two that will help you identify keywords for your online exploration. So, for your library research, enter the topic you want to search into your library's online catalog. You can usually search by both title and subject, and you can try both to see what each search turns up.

If you conduct your research at your school's library, you may want to look for databases in addition to print materials. EBSCO, JSTOR, and ProQuest are some biggies. You can ask your school librarian about them. And if your librarian mentions ERIC when you ask about databases, she or he means the Education Resources Information Center database—not a classmate! Some databases are subject-specific. PubMed, for instance, is a medical database. Databases include journal articles and other scholarly works, which makes them great resources. And the material in databases has been reviewed by experts, such as scientists and professors.

For your Internet research, use one of the major search engines—Google, Bing, Yahoo! Search, or Ask. In the Search bar, type keywords that describe your topic. Consider the following search example as you start your research adventure:

Leukemia

Let's say your topic is a friend who's sick with leukemia. You already know a lot about this topic from a personal perspective—that is, you know what someone with the disease experiences—because you know your friend pretty well. Your friend has told you many details about leukemia and being treated for it. You also have a lot of stuff to tell about yourself and how you feel about knowing someone with cancer. What you don't know a lot about is the science of leukemia. That means you need to research the illness. To turn up useful books and websites, you might use keywords such as "leukemia" or "children with cancer." **A word of warning: Especially when you're researching on the Internet, don't trust just any information that might pop up in your search results. Be sure the source of the information is reliable.** For a topic such as leukemia, the Mayo Clinic, the National Institutes of Health, or other medical or health organizations would be trustworthy sources.

When it comes to books, you can likely trust that much of what you'll find in your library will offer you reliable information. The trick will likely be choosing the most up-to-date resources

WRITE IT OUT!
Research can be a lot of fun, like a treasure hunt. Try going on a mini-research mission. Pick up any book or magazine. Close your eyes, open the publication, and put your finger down anywhere on one of the two pages. Open your eyes and then move your finger to the nearest noun (person, place, or thing). Do some research on that noun. Find out everything you can. Give yourself thirty minutes to investigate. Jot down facts and interesting information. Then go wow someone with your knowledge.

(so you're sure you're finding the latest information about the disease) and weeding out sources that are likely to be less helpful to you. For example, because you aren't a medical professional, a highly technical book may not be the best place to start. On the other hand, a book titled *Patients' and Caregivers' Guide to Leukemia in Children* might be perfect, as it was likely written with the layperson in mind. Similarly, a book for very young children is probably not ideal. Checking it out to get introductory information is fine, but you likely won't want to use the book as one of your main sources. It probably won't have the kind of in-depth information you'll want to write a compelling piece.

Other good sources could be articles. These can come from newspapers, magazines, and even scholarly journals (remember databases?), though this last group might provide information that's more advanced than you need. Still, do a little research and see what comes up. You may, for instance, find a statistic about the occurrence of childhood leukemia that you can use to help your readers understand how many children and families each year go through what your friend is experiencing. You can also look for this information online, but you'll have to be careful about where you look for it. You'll need to assess your online sources.

ASSESSING ONLINE SOURCES

When you search the Internet, you'll likely get a long list of results for each keyword you enter. Before clicking on a result, look at the URL, which is short for uniform resource locator. The URL is the web address of the source, and it can be a rather long string of letters, numbers, and symbols. It reveals important information about the search result, such as the type of site where it's located. Many sites are .com or .org but not all of them. Here's a breakdown of common types of sites:

- .com: <u>com</u>mercial—the objective is to make money, including through advertising, so you're likely to find ads on these sites.
- .org: <u>org</u>anization not for profit—the objective is to help people, but some of these websites might be biased, presenting a very specific viewpoint.
- .edu: <u>edu</u>cational, produced by a school—the objective is to educate.
- .gov: <u>gov</u>ernment, produced by a local, state, or federal government—the objective is to provide information from that level of government, such as laws, guidelines, and resources.

Using the leukemia example, sites ending with .org and .gov will likely be plentiful. The Mayo Clinic's site ends in .org, and so does Kids Health, a site dedicated to providing information about children's health. Cancer.gov and Cancer.org should also be part of the list. The two sites have similar URLs. The first site belongs to the National Cancer Institute, a government agency dedicated to cancer research. The second site is by the American Cancer Society, a national health organization focused on cancer, including prevention, education, and research. All of these sites have helpful, reliable information about leukemia.

Once you find an online source that appears to have good information, check it out further. Look at the publication date, if one is available. Typically, you'll want current information, so look for a recent date—especially if you're writing about a recent event or someone who's living. But if you're looking for background information or resources for a historical topic, a source with an older date might be very useful.

Next, you'll want to know if the author or publisher is trustworthy. To determine this, you might have to do a search on the author or the company that publishes the site. For example, information from the *New York Times*, a respected daily newspaper, would be more reliable than a story from the *National Enquirer,* which publishes sensational stories with sometimes questionable facts. Now look at the contents of the article. Is the article biased? That means it's unreasonably opinionated. Would an expert in the field use and respect this site?

USE WIKIPEDIA AS A STARTING POINT

When thinking about doing Internet research, Wikipedia may come to mind. Some people rely on Wikipedia as a source. The site has articles on all kinds of topics. But Wikipedia is a wiki, which is a website that allows anybody in the world with a computer and Internet access to add, change, or delete the contents of a web page, including you. Right now, you could go into the Wikipedia article on childhood leukemia and change the information. You could put in some "facts" that simply aren't true. You could do so for fun or simply because you have misinformation. People who contribute to Wikipedia's information aren't necessarily experts. And even if some contributors *are* experts, the fact that not all of them are makes the entire site unreliable as a source. But that doesn't mean Wikipedia isn't useful. It can be a great source for other sources.

What do we mean by that? Well, at the end of almost every Wikipedia article is a list of references. These are the sources referred to for information provided in the article. Most of the sources have a link to the original source online, so all you have to do is click on it. Those links are usually not wiki sources, but be sure to check. Often they are **valuable primary (original) sources, or pieces written by people who have experienced what they write about.** For example, if you're writing about the Holocaust in World War II (1939–1945), Anne Frank's diary would be an important primary source because she was a Jewish girl who lived in Europe at that time and wrote the diary herself.

People who heard about or read about a topic somewhere else—that is, instead of experiencing it—write secondary sources, and some references are this type of material. If someone thoroughly researches a topic and then writes an online article about it, that's a secondary source. By using this source, you're taking advantage of that writer's extensive research. Either way, while the material in a Wikipedia article is unreliable, do check out the article's references for possible sources. You might find a gold mine of information.

CONSIDER OTHER RESOURCES

You've looked for websites, books, magazine articles, and maybe even journal articles. Don't stop there! Look for facts about your topic in other places. In addition to exploring books and magazines at a local library branch, keep an open mind to resources such as films, music, and maps. Museums are another great resource. They are repositories of historical items and information just waiting for you to discover them.

Not all research that isn't online requires a field trip. For autobiographical or family narratives, check out family archives. Investigate pictures, scrapbooks, or documents (birth certificates, for example) in your family's possession.

WRITERS ON WRITING

Amy Tan (right) is known for her novel the *Joy Luck Club*, but she also writes nonfiction, including *The Opposite of Fate: Memories of a Writing Life.* Tan is constantly looking for new information on the subjects she writes about. She reads books that provide details about her topics and studies pictures and art to bring her closer to her subject matter. A photograph of her grandmother inspired Tan's writing so much that she carries the image with her wherever she goes.

Karen Grigsby Bates, a writer for National Public Radio, explained Tan's process and its benefits: "Her [abundant] research [for a work she wrote about her family history] gave Tan a fuller understanding of what her grandmother's daily life must have been like in China and broadened her perception of who her grandmother must have been."

INTERVIEW PEOPLE WHO KNOW

Interviewing is another great way to gather information. Think about who was around during the time of your event or who might know about your chosen topic. Going back to the leukemia example, in addition to interviewing your friend, perhaps you could interview your friend's parents or siblings. Those interviews are primary sources, ones you generate yourself.

An interview can be in person, via phone, or by e-mail. Consider who could provide information that would add to the facts you already have and who might make your story more interesting. Write down their names right now. It's time to get ready to do some interviews.

Once you've arranged interviews, prepare for them by writing questions in advance. Write down at least ten questions. **Make sure you ask open-ended questions. These are questions that can't be answered with a simple yes or no. You want questions that will draw out useful information.** If your questions do this, you may end up asking many more than ten questions! The person's answers may spark more questions, and you could end up discussing something about your topic you hadn't even thought of.

Interviewing family members is a great idea for personal narratives. That's because some of them likely experienced your topic with you. The first step is to ask the family member if he or she is comfortable discussing your topic—especially if the topic is something sensitive. If he or she is not, be respectful of that and move on to someone else. When you find a willing interview subject, begin asking him or her your questions and let the conversation flow, allowing the interviewee to share facts and details.

If you're interviewing in person or over the phone, be sure to take notes. And if something your interviewee says really stands out, be careful to write it down exactly as the person said it. If you need to, ask the person to repeat what he or she said. You can

Interviewing family members or researching family history can add detail and depth to a personal narrative story.

explain that you are taking notes. Be careful to keep track of any and all direct quotes by putting quotation marks around them. This will help ensure that you don't accidentally use a direct quote word-for-word in your piece without giving credit to the speaker. Doing so would be plagiarism. If all of this sounds overwhelming, an alternative to note-taking is to record your interview. Recording is a great way to capture exactly what was said. But before recording, be sure to ask your interviewee for permission.

At this point, you'll have gathered a lot of information. You've been collecting pieces of a puzzle. Be careful to keep track of where you found your various facts so you can go back to the sources and get all the information you want or need for your piece.

Research will take time. You might have to make more than one trip to the library. Just remember to be patient and to ask for help if you need it. (Librarians are fantastic resources!) You'll soon have a collection of great sources you can use.

Once your research is done, it's time to chart your course. Get ready to put your narrative together and discover its significance. Ready, set, go!

CHAPTER 3

CHART YOUR COURSE

You've collected a lot of information by now. Of course, gathering facts is only part of the writing process. You still have to connect the dots to transform the facts into a great story. Look at your narrative nonfiction as a journey with a starting place (point A) and a final destination (point B). You'll need to chart your course so you know how you're going to get from point A to point B.

WRITERS ON WRITING
Author John Green (right) offers this advice you might apply to your nonfiction piece: "Tell stories to your friends and pay attention to when they get bored. I still do this a lot, and it helps me understand how to pace a story, and what kind of phrases and images audiences find engaging."

GET THE CHRONOLOGY RIGHT

You can chart your course using different methods. Here are two you can try.

The first method is a timeline. First, grab some construction or notebook paper. Tape the sheets of paper end to end, connecting the short edges. On the far left, jot down where your story begins, the event that goes back the farthest in time. Include at least a date, a place, and the people involved. Label it "Point A."

Next, go to the other end of your timeline, the right side, and write down the last event of your story. List how, when, and where your story ends. Label it "Point B." Use point B to tell why this story is significant. Consider these questions:

- Why is the experience important to you, or why might it matter to your readers?
- What did you—or what will your readers—learn from the experience?
- How did the events change your life, the people in the story, or history?
- How might your piece appeal to or help someone?

Be specific. The rest of your story (the middle part) depends on this information. Every part of your story will build up to the important message of your story.

For the rest of your timeline, fill in all the events that happened between point A and point B. Make sure they're in chronological order. Add exact dates if you know them. Leave space for entries to grow as you go. If you're writing a personal piece, you'll probably think of more details as you write. If your piece isn't autobiographical, you'll do more research to find more details.

The second method is an outline. To make your outline, you can use paper and pen or pencil, or you can use an electronic device. An outline is simply a list of the information you want to include in your piece. Think of it as a sort of vertical version of a timeline. The list doesn't include every detail you've uncovered in your research. Rather, it's a skeleton to get you started. Outlines are laid out in a hierarchy, with main ideas listed first and smaller ideas or details listed below each main idea. If you want, you can use Roman numerals, numbers, or letters to organize your outline. For example, Roman numerals I, II, and III could represent main ideas and the letters *A*, *B*, and *C* under each main idea could represent smaller ideas.

For each of the events in the middle, add details that will bring the story to life. **In addition to who, what, where, when, why, and how, think about the senses. What did people see, hear, smell, taste, or touch?** Getting some of this kind of information down now will be helpful when you start writing. You'll have it right there, ready to incorporate into your story rather than having to go searching for it.

CHOOSE WHAT TO USE

After charting your course, you may find that all the details won't be necessary to tell your story well. Next, you'll choose which events to use and which to leave out. If you created an outline electronically, print it.

Get three colored markers, highlighters, pencils, or crayons. With the first color, circle all the most important events on your timeline or in your outline. These are the details that are so essential that your story would be pointless or incomplete without them. With the second colored writing utensil, circle the events that point to your lesson, the part that changed your life (for good or bad) or will make the story meaningful to readers. Some of your events may have two colored circles. That's OK. These items are important to your story *and* hint at the lesson or meaning.

LEARN FROM THE MASTERS

Anne Frank: The Diary of a Young Girl is an excellent example of a book written in the first person. In her diary, Anne, a Jewish girl hiding with her family from the Nazis, tells the story of her experiences in World War II through her own eyes. Readers know what Anne sees, hears, smells,

and experiences as she hides. Her writing allows readers into her deepest thoughts and emotions. In one particularly reflective passage, Anne says: "Although I'm only fourteen, I know quite well what I want, I know who is right and who is wrong. I have my opinions, my own ideas and principles, and although it may sound pretty mad from an adolescent, I feel more of a person than a child, I feel quite independent of anyone."

Anne Frank (above) wrote her diary while in hiding from the Nazis.

With your third colored utensil, circle items that are important or interesting but not essential. This last group is what you can leave out of your narrative (if you want).

SELECT A POINT OF VIEW

Another important decision is choosing the narrator, or deciding who will tell your story. In writing, this is called point of view (POV). There are three POVs: first person, second person, and third person.

If you tell your own story, that's the first-person POV. Readers will "hear" you telling your own tale, and you'll often use the pronoun *I*. A great deal of narrative nonfiction is written in the first person. John Steinbeck's nonfiction book *Travels with Charley: In Search of America* is a great example of first-person POV:

> *When I was very young and the urge to be someplace else was on me, I was assured by mature people that maturity would cure this itch. When years described me as mature, the remedy prescribed was middle age. In middle age I was assured that greater age would calm my fever and now that I am fifty-eight perhaps senility will do the job. Nothing has worked.*

Second-person POV is often used in magazine and newspaper articles, manuals, and how-to books. The author addresses the reader as "you." Second-person POV isn't used very often in narrative nonfiction.

Third-person POV means an unknown or neutral narrator tells the story. The narrator is not you and not another character in the story. It's an unknown being who always knows what's going on. Third-person is the POV best suited for narrative nonfiction that isn't autobiographical. Be careful not to use the pronoun *I* in third-person POV.

Langston Hughes, a famous poet, was very passionate about history and brought historical events to life through narrative nonfiction. The nonfiction book *Fight for Freedom and Other Writings on Civil Rights* shows his third-person writing style:

> *Other slaves were scarcely on shore before they began to plan their escape. Some ran away from the southern plantations and joined the [American] Indians in the swamps. Others just ran, without knowing where they were going. The runaways were pursued by*

slave-catchers with dogs. . . . It was inevitable that secret organizations of slaves came into existence whose whispered objective was freedom.

Once you've decided which POV to use for your piece, you're ready to write. Keep reading to learn how to get your first draft on paper!

CHAPTER 4

WRITE SOMETHING—EVEN IF IT'S BAD!

With all the prewriting work done, you're ready to write a terrible draft of your narrative nonfiction—yes, we said terrible! That's because if you don't let yourself make mistakes and write badly, you may never put a word on the page. You might have writer's block forever, thinking you have to get every word perfect on your first try.

NO PERFECTIONISM ALLOWED

To get started writing your terrible draft, simply pound out an introduction to your piece, weaving together facts you found in your research. Don't worry at all about how the words look or sound. But do remember to avoid plagiarism. Be careful to write the facts in your own words. It's not OK to use someone else's sentence and just change a few words. Your sentences must be completely original. If you do include another's words in your introduction—or anywhere in your piece—make sure to put quotation marks around them, and mention in your writing to whom the words belong.

Other than this rule, don't fret about the details right now. You will have plenty of time later to think about spelling and grammar. For now, just start writing!

TRY A CLIFF-HANGER

Although *anything* you write at the drafting stage is fine, some writers still find it helpful to have some general guidelines to go on. If that applies to you, keep reading. One good rule to follow (for those who like to follow rules!) is that you can rarely go wrong with a cliff-hanger introduction. It snatches readers out of their seat, getting their attention from the get-go. High school teacher Erin Gruwell wrote a book about her experiences as a teacher and made great use of the cliff-hanger introduction. At the beginning of her book, *The Freedom Writers Diary: How a Teacher and 150 Teens Used Writing to Change Themselves and the World around Them*, she used this diary entry from one student to grab her readers' attention:

> *Dear Diary,*
>
> *I always thought that "odd" was a three-letter word; but today I found out it has seven, and they spell G-r-u-w-e-l-l. My freshman English teacher is way out there. I wonder how she got this job. The administration should have known better than to give her this class, but I guess she didn't know any better than to take it. How is she going to handle four classes full of this school's rejects? Most people at this school doubt that we can even read or write.*

Doesn't that make you want to read more? A simple student diary entry pulls readers into the world of a freshman English class and makes you wonder about this teacher, leaving you curious to learn more about her and the students.

If you go with a cliff-hanger introduction, don't reveal too much information. And definitely don't give away the ending (or the middle). Give your readers just enough to leave them hanging and wanting more. That's what a cliff-hanger introduction is meant to do.

PACE YOUR STORY

Once you've drafted your introduction, take a break. Walk away from it for a while and do something else. When you come back, think about all you've accomplished:

- You've chosen a topic.
- You've done your research.
- You've made a timeline or an outline—or maybe both.
- You've chosen which events to include.
- You've selected a POV.
- You've gotten past writer's block.
- You've written an introduction.

You've made excellent strides in writing narrative nonfiction. Keep going. Tell the rest of your fascinating story. Put your timeline or outline in plain sight, maybe taped to the wall. Number the events in the order you plan to tell about them.

You can write your story in strict chronological order, from beginning to end, or you can start in the middle or even near the end and use the flashback technique, mixing up the order.

Flashback interrupts the story and tells about previous events that are important to the facts. For example, the scene might be set at sundown in a damp forest under a cover of bristly pines and white-barked cedars. To explain your paralyzing fear of the approaching darkness, you have to go back and tell readers what happened when you were four years old to make you afraid of the dark.

That's when flashback is effective. The readers are with you in the forest, sharing your fear, but then you take them back to a certain incident so they'll understand why you're really afraid. Switch to verbs in the past tense while in flashback mode. Use flashback only if the events of the past are necessary to understand the rest of the narrative.

WRITERS ON WRITING

John McPhee (below) is a nonfiction writer who won the Pulitzer Prize for General Nonfiction in 1999 for his five-book collection *Annals of the Former World*. In an interview, McPhee described his story as a journey and admitted that starting at the beginning of that journey doesn't always work for him: "What if you started telling the piece of writing further down the river, I wondered. That way, when you get to the end of the trip, you're really only halfway through the story. What you do then is switch to the past tense, creating a flashback, and you back up and start your trip over again."

USE THE SENSES

As you write your narrative nonfiction, you'll likely picture scenes in your head. Your memory saves facts. It also preserves pictures, sounds, and smells. Your brain also stores how something felt when you touched it or what someone said years ago. If you're writing about history, you've probably visualized battle scenes or sunken ships or interesting people.

Your readers haven't experienced what you've experienced, so help them visualize what's in your mind. Describe each scene to them in detail using the five senses in your writing. For example, don't simply write that you're driving past a dairy farm on a cloudy day. Describe how the cows smell. Explain how the sky looks and what shapes the clouds are making. Write about what you hear, such as the squawk of birds, the *rat-a-tat-tat* of rain on the car roof, or the mind-numbing sound of the car's tires on the road. This applies to writing nonpersonal narratives too. Set the scene. Help the readers experience the event you're writing about.

Here's an example. Author Esmeralda Santiago used the senses to describe eating an unripe guava in *When I Was Puerto Rican: A Memoir*:

> *A green guava is sour and hard. You bite into it at its widest point, because it's easier to grasp with your teeth. You hear the skin, meat, and seeds crunching inside your head, while the inside of your mouth explodes in little spurts of sour.*

Another way to invite your readers to hear what's going on in your story is to use dialogue. But be careful! Remember that narrative nonfiction must be completely true, so don't make up dialogue or what two people could have said to each other. Use dialogue in an autobiographical piece only if you remember what someone said word for word.

USE LITERARY TECHNIQUES

Another way to create a fascinating scene is to use literary techniques, which include simile, metaphor, alliteration, repetition, and personification. Similes and metaphors show how one thing is like something else. A simile uses the word *like* or *as*, such as "He was like a cat moving swiftly and with great agility." A metaphor is a word or phrase that suggests how unrelated things are alike. "That girl is a night owl" is an example. The girl isn't actually a night owl. Rather, she's awake at night the way an owl is.

Alliteration is when words near one another begin with the same letter or sound. Tongue twisters often use alliteration. Here's an example: She sells seashells by the seashore. Personification is giving something that's nonhuman human qualities, which makes it seem like a person.

John Steinbeck used simile, alliteration, and personification in "Flight," a short story:

> *The farm buildings huddled like little clinging aphids*
> *on the mountain skirts, crouched low to the ground*
> *as though the wind might blow them into the sea. . . .*
> *Five-fingered ferns hung over the water and dropped*
> *spray from their fingertips.*

The first part of the quote above is an example of simile. In the second part of the quote, "Five-fingered ferns" is an example of both alliteration and personification. Notice how all the words begin with the letter *f*. And as a type of plant, ferns don't have fingers, but people do, and describing ferns as having five fingers makes them humanlike.

In his famous "I Have a Dream" speech, Martin Luther King Jr. relied on repetition of "one hundred years later" to make his point:

> *But one hundred years later, the Negro still is not free.*
> *One hundred years later, the life of the Negro is still*
> *sadly crippled by the manacles of segregation and the*
> *chains of discrimination. One hundred years later, the*
> *Negro lives on a lonely island of poverty in the midst*
> *of a vast ocean of material prosperity. One hundred*
> *years later, the Negro is still languished in the corners*
> *of American society and finds himself an exile in his*
> *own land. And so we've come here today to dramatize a*
> *shameful condition.*

MAKE IT USEFUL

You're making facts come to life with rich descriptions and literary techniques. Next, discover why your story is useful. Here are some things to remember about writing useful narrative nonfiction:

- It must have a purpose.
- It might help you (or someone else) heal from past hurts or tragedies.
- It could help you and others understand life or the world better.
- It brings meaning to life or to history.
- It doesn't cover your whole life—it focuses on a meaningful life-changing event.
- It's not only about events. It's about why those events are important.

Once you decide the specific purpose of your narrative, write it down. Then add some hints to what you've written. Don't come right out and tell what your lesson or the meaning is. Instead, let your readers discover the lesson from hints you give throughout your well-told story. By the time you end your narrative nonfiction, readers will be ready to think about why the story is useful.

END IT WELL

Every writer ends a story differently. Some end it with exciting or shocking facts or an unexpected conclusion. An effective ending might reveal something you've never told anyone because you trust your readers to share your thoughts and, perhaps, your secrets. An ending like this can make a great impression on a reader. Other writers end a story quietly, letting readers think about how the story speaks to them personally. This type of ending too can have a tremendous impact.

When writing your conclusion, think about what you or the main people in your story learned or what your reader might learn from the event. How did the people change? How did the people or the event change history? How did the event or history change you? However you conclude your narrative nonfiction, in addition to making it useful, make it significant. Be sure it has an emotional effect.

As you craft your ending, be careful to not simply summarize your story. Instead, connect the ending to the beginning. And consider how you can make your last sentence memorable. Don't worry about writing the perfect ending now. Remember, you're just getting some words on paper. Once you've drafted the entire piece, you'll be ready to move on to the next step, where you'll review and revise.

WRITE IT OUT!
A good way to learn how to add personal meaning to a story is by practicing. One by one, create one sentence that tells what each of the following items means to you:

- Clothes
- A day in the woods
- A 6-inch (15-centimeter) fish
- My brother or sister
- Thunderstorms

REVIEW AND REVISE

You've finished your draft. Celebrate! Getting something down on paper is an enormous step. The next step is to review it. Then you'll revise it, including adding more literary techniques and cleaning up elements such as transitions, grammar, and spelling. You'll have someone else read your work too. Getting a fresh perspective is an important part of the revising process.

EVALUATE YOUR NARRATIVE

The best way to evaluate what you've written is to read it out loud. Find a quiet place, and then read your story from beginning to end, without stopping. Reading aloud alerts you to elements that don't make sense or sound right, from words to sentences to entire paragraphs.

When you're finished, highlight the areas that need work. Don't be surprised if you end up highlighting much of your draft. Remember, you had the freedom to write badly.

After you've highlighted areas to revise, change them one at a time. Revise, rewrite, revise, and rewrite again until a section makes sense and sounds great to you. During the revision process, you may read a section—or just one sentence—out loud several times until you're satisfied with it.

This process will take some time. This is your work of art. Refine your story and improve your writing until you can step back and say with confidence that it's a piece you feel proud of.

DEVELOP PLACES AND PEOPLE

Read the description of one of your scenes. Will the reader see, hear, and maybe smell or taste what you're describing? Will the reader feel what's going on? If not, add details and include colorful, interesting words. Add word variety by using a thesaurus. It will help you transform ordinary words into vivid language. Find as many ordinary words as you can in your story and replace them with interesting synonyms. The following table has some examples:

Suggestions for Making the Ordinary Extraordinary	
Ordinary word	Synonyms
Cloudy	Overcast, hazy, dull, gloomy
Green	Emerald, lime, olive
Small	Miniature, tiny, wee, minuscule
Fast	Rapid, swift, quick, speedy
Walk	Stroll, amble, stagger, wander
Talk	Discuss, chat, babble, gab
Dark	Murky, gloomy, mysterious, dim
Windy	Breezy, gusty, blustery
Dog	Pooch, canine, pup, mutt
Road	Path, boulevard, lane, avenue

Next, examine the people in your story. Add descriptive language so readers get to know those people personally. Reveal those people's thoughts and feelings. Maybe you need to tell the reader more about you, the author. Don't be afraid to share your thoughts and feelings, as doing so will strengthen the deeper meaning of your narrative.

ADD MORE LITERARY TECHNIQUES

You can also improve your writing by adding more literary techniques. You already know some of them, such as simile, metaphor, alliteration, personification, and repetition. Assonance and onomatopoeia are other techniques. Assonance is sort of like alliteration, except it's the repetition of vowel sounds. You can have a lot of fun with onomatopoeia, which are words that imitate a sound, such as *hiss* or *plop*. And don't forget the five senses and cliff-hangers. Using literary techniques, rewrite sentences or paragraphs to make them more interesting.

Examples of Literary Techniques at Work	
Ordinary details	Interesting descriptions (literary techniques)
The trip was very expensive.	The trip ate up fifty-dollar bills at the gas pump and stole hundreds at tattered hotels. (personification)
The land and the sky were beautiful.	The raw land and ever-changing sky were like a fantasy. (simile)
The sound of the tires and the wind made me sleepy.	The humming tires and whistling wind constantly called me, beckoning me to return to the days I had forgotten long ago. (onomatopoeia, alliteration, assonance, and personification)
I've always wanted to go back to that peaceful place.	That place is my paradise. I'd go back tomorrow to stare at deformed mountains, smell rotten fish, listen to angry waters, taste the salt air, and feel the rock-hard shells of snow-white crabs. (metaphor, repetition, five senses)
But for some reason, I'm afraid.	But there's a memory that haunts me. It's what turned that incredible journey into an ugly twist of fate. (cliff-hanger)

Now do the same thing with the people in your story. Describe them with vivid language. Be sure to use literary techniques.

INCLUDE TRANSITION SENTENCES

When evaluating your writing, look out for bumps and jumps. Thoughts, ideas, and scenes should move smoothly from one to the next.

Transition sentences make that happen. A transition sentence effortlessly moves readers to something new. Here's an example: *A week later, we'd have to live through the same dark nightmare again. But next time, it would be worse.* The second sentence sets up the next time, moving readers from "a week later" to that next time.

POLISH THE GRAMMAR

Grammar is next. You may have cleaned up some of it already, but now it's time to do some serious fine-tuning. In his book *Fumblerules: A Lighthearted Guide to Grammar and Good Usage*, William Safire included a humorous, helpful list of grammar rules. In the list, he describes each rule by breaking it. He calls these rules "never-say-neverisms." Here's a selection of them:

- Avoid run-on sentences they are hard to read.
- Don't use no double negatives.
- Reserve the apostrophe for it's proper use and omit it when its not needed.
- Verbs has to agree with their subjects.
- No sentence fragments.
- Proofread carefully to see if you any words out.
- Avoid commas, that are not necessary.
- Don't overuse exclamation marks!!!

If you didn't already catch the errors, here's a corrected list:

- Avoid run-on sentences. They are hard to read.
- Don't use double negatives.
- Reserve the apostrophe for its proper use and omit it when it's not needed.
- Verbs have to agree with their subjects.
- Don't use sentence fragments.
- Proofread carefully to see if you left any words out.
- Avoid commas that are not necessary.
- Don't overuse exclamation marks.

Also, keep an eye out for words you may have mixed up—for example, using *your* instead of *you're*. Here's a table of words to keep an eye out for as you revise:

Some of the Most Commonly Confused Words			
Word	Meaning	Word	Meaning
Hear	To sense through the ear	To	In the direction of
Here	At this place	Too	Also; excessively
Their	Belonging to people or things	Two	A number; the sum of one plus one
There	At or in a certain place	Who's	Contraction for "who is"
They're	Contraction for "they are"	Whose	Belonging to a certain person
Its	Belonging to a thing	Your	Belonging to a person or people
It's	Contraction for "it is"	You're	Contraction for "you are"

As you revise, watch your comma use. Using commas correctly takes practice. Use them in the following places:

- In a list. Separate *all* items in a list with commas. Here's an example: The Popsicle flavors are cherry, grape, orange, and lime. Notice the comma before the conjunction and. That's called a serial comma. Some grammarians say you need it. Some say you don't. Most teachers are in favor of it, so that's why you're safest to include it.

- After an introductory word or phrase. If you start a sentence with an introductory word such as *however*, follow the word with a comma. The same applies to a phrase such as "The next day" or "In the meantime." Example 1: However, the storm did not last long. Example 2: Although we were extremely full, we ate the hamburgers anyway.

- Between two independent clauses separated by a conjunction. An independent clause is a group of words that can stand alone as a complete sentence (it has a noun and a verb). When you join two independent clauses with a conjunction such as *or*, *and*, or *but*, you have a complex sentence. To test if you need a comma, read the clauses on both sides of the conjunction. If they can both stand alone, you have a complex sentence. If that's the case, put a comma before the conjunction. Here's an example: We had French toast and bacon for breakfast, but our friends had pancakes.

Pay attention to apostrophes too. In addition to using them in contractions, remember to use an apostrophe and the letter *s* for possessives, which is when something belongs to someone or

something. Here are some examples: the dog's food, my sister's car, and the birds' nest (there's more than one bird). Caution: There's one exception to this. The word *its* is a possessive, but it doesn't have an apostrophe. You'd write, "The company published its annual report," *not* "The company published it's annual report." This information about *its* and *it's* is in the table about commonly confused words, but we're repeating it because it's really important!

There's more to learn, but conquer these first. Go through your narrative nonfiction specifically to find errors in grammar and punctuation. But at the same time, you don't want to get too bogged down. So try to make it fun, like one of those search-and-find games!

PROVIDE REFERENCES

OK, you're getting closer to being done. If you used someone else's words in your piece, you have some additional work to do. For each quote in your nonfiction narrative, add a footnote and a reference, which shows where you found the material. For example, if you quote text from a book, the reference would include the author's name, the title of the book, the publisher's location and name, and the page number where the quoted material appears.

Depending on the audience you're writing for, the way the publication information is formatted will vary. But all references should contain enough information for your readers to find the quoted material themselves. Even if they never double-check your quotes, taking this step gives your piece extra credibility.

GET FEEDBACK

You've approached your draft with an editorial eye and revised, reworked, and rewritten. You're in the final stretch. You're about to cross the finish line on this incredible writing journey and go public with your story. Find at least one set of ears to listen to you as you read it out loud. Parents, grandparents, brothers, sisters, and best friends are all great candidates.

When you've finished reading, ask them to tell you what was great about your story and what you need to improve. Find out if they were confused by anything. Ask if there's something they'd like to know more about. After you get their feedback, use it to make more changes.

Finally, find someone who writes well. If the person's good with grammar, that's even better. Ask that person to read your narrative nonfiction, mark the errors, and write suggestions in the margins.

Next, take the copy he or she marked up and revise one last time. Give your story a final polish. That's it—you've done it! You've written a narrative nonfiction piece that's true, informative, interesting, and even inspirational. You've taken facts and made them read like fiction. Your scenes are vivid, the people are real, and your story has a purpose.

Congratulations on a true story well told! Well done!

WRITE IT OUT!

The best way to learn how to revise is to do it—so practice revising! Find a book, any book. Or look at a magazine or newspaper article. Pick out two or three sentences and change them, making them better. Use language that is more vivid than what was published. Add literary techniques. Develop the scene. Dig more deeply into the people in the story. Then compare the original version with yours. Read them to someone and find out what that person thinks of your changes. Ask what he or she would have done differently.

WRITING FOR A LIVING

Are you interested in being a professional writer—either now or in the future? If so, the possibilities for writing narrative nonfiction professionally are numerous. Becoming a narrative nonfiction book author is one way to make a living doing this type of writing. To get started down this path, you'll want to send a manuscript and a cover letter to as many publishers as you can. In a cover letter to a publisher, you explain why your story is different from others already in bookstores or on the Internet. You'll want to convince the publisher that people need your story and will want to buy it and read it.

Another route to take if you want to write narrative nonfiction professionally is journalism. A journalist writes articles for magazines, newspapers, and websites. Many journalists present facts, news, history, science, and technology in creative, engaging ways. Journalists often write in a narrative nonfiction style. Personal-interest stories and descriptive writing about places could be a great fit. If you'd like to become such a journalist, a good way to get started is to write a news story. Pay attention to what's happening in your school or community and write an interesting article about it. Remember, your article should have a deeper meaning than regular news. Next, submit it to your school newspaper, your local newspaper, or a magazine. Don't give up if your article is rejected a few times. You'll need persistence to get your first article published. Once you start getting published, be sure to save copies of the articles. These are called clips. Take your collection of clips with you when you interview with publishers about writing jobs.

Yet another option for aspiring narrative nonfiction writers is the business world. Plenty of companies and organizations want writers to create articles, information, or creative news for their websites. The creative style of narrative nonfiction can make ordinary companies and products very interesting. Companies are looking for original, creative people to make their businesses look good. To apply for a job as a writer with a company, you might try submitting a well-written snippet about the company with your application. Impress them with your knowledge of their business and your interesting style of writing. Show the company how your writing engages readers and makes them want to read more. When you get an interview, bring your portfolio of clips with you. Getting your work published in print or online is an important part of breaking into a writing career, so start now. Write something interesting and submit it to some appropriate businesses or publishers.

An array of opportunities exists if you dream of having a writing career. With determination, hard work, and dedication to honing your writing skills, you can make a living from writing narrative nonfiction.

SOURCE NOTES

4   John Green, "Ideas and Inspiration Questions," *John Green* (blog), accessed December 16, 2014, http://johngreenbooks.com/ideas -questions/.

5   Lee Gutkind, "What Is Creative Nonfiction?," *Creative Nonfiction*, accessed December 16, 2014, https://www.creativenonfiction.org /what-is-creative-nonfiction.

6   Ray Suarez, *Latino Americans: The 500-Year Legacy That Shaped a Nation* (New York: Celebra, 2013), *Google Books*, accessed January 7, 2015, https://books.google.com/books?id=TwJF1rI-Zv8C&printsec=frontc over#v=onepage&q&f=false.

7   "Behind the Book: *The Glass Castle* by Jeannette Walls," Simon & Schuster, accessed December 16, 2014, http://books.simonandschuster .com/Glass-Castle/Jeannette-Walls/9781439156964/behind_the_ book?tab_index=0.

8   Joan Didion, *The Year of Magical Thinking* (New York: Vintage, 2007), 3.

9   William Least Heat-Moon, "William Least Heat-Moon: Interview with Hank Nuwer; 'The Road to Serendipity,'" Hank Nuwer, accessed December 16, 2014, http://www.hanknuwer.com/William%20 Least%20Heat%20Moon%20(Trogdon).html.

19 Karen Grigsby Bates, "Amy Tan Weaves Family Mystery into 'Valley of Amazement,'" *NPR*, November 4, 2013, http://www.npr.org/blogs /codeswitch/2013/11/04/242926707/amy-tan-weaves-family-mystery -into-valley-of-amazement.

22 John Green, "Biographical Questions," *John Green* (blog), accessed December 16, 2014, http://johngreenbooks.com/biographical -questions/.

25 Anne Frank, "The Diary of a Young Girl Quotes," *Goodreads*, accessed December 16, 2014, https://www.goodreads.com/work /quotes/3532896-het-achterhuis.

26 John Steinbeck, *Travels with Charley: In Search of America* (New York: Bantam, 1961), 3.

26–27   Langston Hughes, *Fight for Freedom and Other Writings on Civil Rights* (Columbia: University of Missouri Press, 2001), 34.

29   Erin Gruwell, *The Freedom Writers Diary: How a Teacher and 150 Teens Used Writing to Change Themselves and the World around Them* (New York: Broadway, 2009), 6.

31   Peter Hessler, "John McPhee, The Art of Nonfiction No. 3," *Paris Review*, accessed December 16, 2014, http://www.theparisreview.org /interviews/5997/the-art-of-nonfiction-no-3-john-mcphee.

32   Esmeralda Santiago, *When I Was Puerto Rican: A Memoir* (Cambridge, MA: Da Capo, 1993), 3.

33   John Steinbeck, "Flight," in *The Portable Steinbeck*, ed., Pascal Covici Jr. (New York: Penguin, 1935), *Google Books*, accessed December 16, 2014, https://books.google.com/books?id=3oxHAVhy1bI C&lpg=PT80&dq=The%20farm%20buildings%20huddled%20 like%20the%20clinging%20aphids%20on%20the%20mountain%20 skirts&pg=PT80#v=onepage&q=The%20farm%20buildings%20 huddled%20like%20the%20clinging%20aphids%20on%20the%20 mountain%20skirts&f=true.

33   Martin Luther King Jr., "I Have a Dream" speech, August 28, 1963, *American Rhetoric Top 100 Speeches*, accessed December 16, 2014, http://www.americanrhetoric.com/speeches/mlkihaveadream.htm.

37   Emily Temple, "'My Pencils Outlast Their Erasers': Great Writers on the Art of Revision," *Atlantic*, January 14, 2013, http://www.theatlantic .com/entertainment/archive/2013/01/my-pencils-outlast-their-erasers -great-writers-on-the-art-of-revision/267011/2/.

40   William Safire, "Quotes about Grammar," in the *New York Times*, November 4, 1979, also available in *Fumblerules: A Lighthearted Guide to Grammar and Good Usage*, accessed October 24, 2014, *Goodreads*, https://www.goodreads.com/quotes/tag/grammar?page=2.

43   Richard Nordquist, "Toni Morrison on Writing," *About Education*, accessed October 24, 2014, http://grammar.about.com/od /advicefromthepros/a/morrisinterview.htm.

GLOSSARY

cathartic: to cause to release emotions

chronological: arranged in the order that things happened

editor: someone who revises writing to make it clearer and to correct spelling and grammar

flashback: part of a story that describes something that happened in the past

genre: a category of literature characterized by a particular style or content

plagiarism: using someone else's words or ideas as your own

point of view: the perspective from which a story is told

thesaurus: a book that lists words with the same or similar meaning in groups

wordsmith: a person who uses words skillfully

writer's block: a condition in which emotions such as anxiety or fear leave a writer unable to proceed with a piece of writing

SELECTED BIBLIOGRAPHY

Green, John. "Biographical Questions." *John Green* (blog). Accessed December 16, 2014. http://johngreenbooks.com /biographical-questions/.

Gutkind, Lee. "What Is Creative Nonfiction?" *Creative Nonfiction*. Accessed December 16, 2014. https://www .creativenonfiction.org.

Least Heat-Moon, William. *Blue Highways: A Journey into America*, (New York: Back Bay, 1999).

Safire, William. "Quotes about Grammar." In the *New York Times*, November 4, 1979. Also available in *Fumblerules: A Lighthearted Guide to Grammar and Good Usage*. Goodreads. Accessed October 24, 2014. https://www.goodreads.com /quotes/tag/grammar?page=2

Walls, Jeannette. *The Glass Castle: A Memoir* (New York: Scribner, 2005).

FURTHER INFORMATION

Bell, James Scott. *How to Make a Living as a Writer*. Woodland Hills, CA: Compendium, 2014. Check out this book for a wealth of information on becoming a successful professional writer, including writing in different genres, editing your own work, and managing your time.

Bodden, Valerie. *Write and Revise Your Project*. Minneapolis: Lerner Publications, 2015. This book offers helpful advice for creating awesome research papers and presentations.

Fogarty, Mignon. *Grammar Girl Presents the Ultimate Writing Guide for Students*. New York: Henry Holt, 2011. Make revisions and grammar fun with this guide to many types of writing.

———. *Grammar Girl's Quick and Dirty Tips for Better Writing*. New York: Henry Holt, 2008. Use this fun book to learn about grammar painlessly.

Go Teen Writers
http://goteenwriters.blogspot.com
This blog offers tips, connections, and encouragement for young writers.

Grammar Girl

> http://www.quickanddirtytips.com/grammar-girl
> Refer to this website for a fun, easy way to find answers to
> your questions about grammar.

Oliver, Laura. *The Story Within: New Insights and Inspiration for
Writers*. New York: Alpha, 2011. This book offers great ideas
and inspiration for writing a memoir.

Truss, Lynne. *Eats, Shoots & Leaves: The Zero Tolerance Approach
to Punctuation*. New York: Gotham, 2008. This book gives
helpful, entertaining answers to your punctuation questions.

Vander Hook, Sue. *Writing Intriguing Informational Pieces*.
Minneapolis: Lerner Publications, 2016. Learn how to craft
interesting writing that informs, from deciding on a topic and
researching it to writing a first draft and refining your work.

INDEX

PHOTO ACKNOWLEDGMENTS

The images in this book are used with the permission of: © Lynn Goldsmith/CORBIS, p. 7; © Basso Cannarsa/LUZphoto/Redux, p. 9; © iStockphoto.com/GlobalIP, p. 12; © Vichy Deal/Shutterstock.com, p. 11; © Mark Von Holden/WireImage/Getty Images, p. 19; © Jose Luis Pelaez Inc/Getty Images, p. 21; © Alexander Tamargo/Getty Images, p. 22; © AP Photo/Anne Frank Center/CORBIS, p. 25; © iStockphoto.com/Danny Hooks, p. 27; AP Photo/Charles Rex Arbogast, p. 31; © SARAWUTK/Shutterstock.com, p. 32; © Dan Thornberg/Shutterstock.com, p. 35; © Horst Tharpe/Hulton Archive/Getty Images, p. 37; © aluxum/Shutterstock.com, p. 42; © Jeremy Sutton-Hibbert/Alamy, p. 43; © koosen/Shutterstock.com (cardboard background); © Everything/Shutterstock.com (spiral notebook); © AtthameeNi/Shutterstock.com (grid paper); © oleschwantder/Shutterstock.com (yellow lined paper).

Cover: © koosen/Shutterstock.com (cardboard); © oleschwantder/Shutterstcock.com (yellow lined paper).

ABOUT THE AUTHOR

Sue Vander Hook is the author of more than forty books, including biographies and books on writing, technology, sports, disease, and historical events. "My passion," Vander Hook says, "is to make the world exciting and interesting to young readers. I enjoy bringing history to life and creating scenes that readers can 'see' and experience. It is my privilege to pass along writing tips to young writers who have a story to tell and need the encouragement to write it down." She has a master's degree in English studies from Minnesota State University, Mankato, where she also taught writing.